FOREST BOOKS

THE NAKED MACHINE

MATTÍAS JOHANNESSEN was born in Reykjavik on 3rd January 1930. Educated at the universities of Iceland and Copenhagen, he graduated in Icelandic literature and in 1952 began his distinguished career as a journalist with Iceland's leading newspaper, *Morgunblaðið*. Within seven years he became their chief editor. His first book was published in 1958, and in the same year he published his first volume of poetry. Since that time he has written more than thirty volumes including novels, plays, short stories and poetry. He has been a leading figure in the cultural life of Iceland and in 1983 he was awarded the Icelandic Language Foundation Prize. He is now acknowledged as one of their greatest poets and his poetry has been translated into many languages. However, this is the first volume of his work in English.

MARSHALL BREMENT was born in New York City in 1932 and was educated at Brooklyn College and the University of Maryland. As a diplomat he became fluent in eight languages, one of which is Icelandic. During his career he has won many awards for distinguished public service and is the author of many 'in-house' publications. While American Ambassador for Iceland, he translated and edited a book of modern Icelandic poetry which was published by the Icelandic Review Press in 1985. He also writes poetry himself and is married to the novelist Pamela Sanders.

THE
NAKED MACHINE

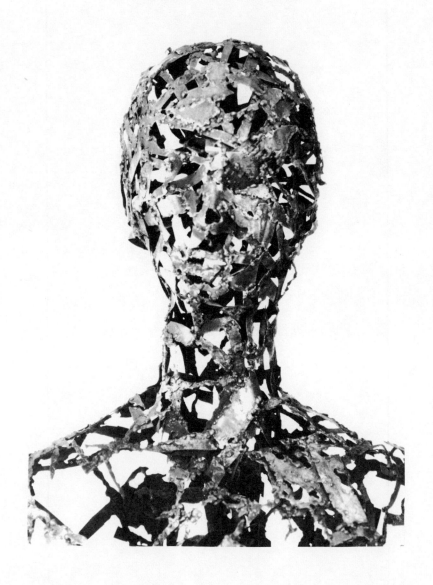

For Haya Glauberman

and for Hanna and Pamela

THE
NAKED MACHINE

SELECTED POEMS
by
MATTHÍAS JOHANNESSEN

Illustrated by
MANFRED FISCHER

With photographs by
KATRIN MEINERT

ALMENNA BÓKAFÉLAGIÐ
REYKJAVÍK

FOREST BOOKS
LONDON ☆ 1988 ☆ BOSTON

PUBLISHED BY
FOREST BOOKS
20 Forest View, Chingford, London E4 7AY, U.K.
61 Lincoln Road, Wayland, MA 01788, U.S.A.
and
ALMENNA BÓKAFÉLAGIÐ
P.O. Box 9, Austurstraeti 18, 121 Reykjavík, Iceland

First published 1988

Typeset in Great Britain by Cover to Cover, Cambridge
Printed in Great Britain by A. Wheaton & Co. Ltd, Exeter

Translations © Marshall Brement
Icelandic text © Matthías Johannessen
Photographs © Katrin Meinert
Illustrations & sculpture © Manfred Fischer

British Library Cataloguing in Publication Data:
Johannessen, Matthías
The Naked Machine: Selected Poems of
Matthías Johannessen.
1. English poetry——Translations from
Icelandic.
I. Title   II. Brement, Marshall
839'.6914   PT7511.J534

ISBN 0–948259–44–2 Cased
ISBN 0–948259–43–4 Paperback

Library of Congress Catalogue Card No.:

87–083425

Matthías Johannessen

Contents

Introduction

In the past twenty-five years Matthías Johannessen has published more than thirty volumes of poetry, plays, biography, history, literary essays and art criticism. Six of his plays have been produced on the Reykjavík stage, television and radio. This body of work was written while he was concurrently editor-in-chief and a constant contributor to Iceland's major daily newspaper. The author of thousands of pages of prose, Johannessen nevertheless has always considered himself first and foremost a poet.

Both as an individual and a writer, he is sharply differentiated from the majority of his Icelandic artistic contemporaries by the consistent conservatism of his politics and his profoundly religious outlook. Since most Icelandic writers are agnostic and on the left of the political spectrum, his views have exposed him to the sharpest possible aesthetic scrutiny and criticism by those who disagree with him politically. But even his most acerbic critics are forced to acknowledge his extraordinary qualities. If nothing else, he is certainly one of the most prolific writers of his generation anywhere.

Matthías Johannessen was born in Reykjavík on 3 January 1930. His grandfather, also named Matthías Johannessen, was a merchant from Bergen in Norway and came to Iceland in the mid-nineteenth century, married, and settled here. He founded the first shop in Reykjavík specializing in women's accessories.

The poet's maternal grandfather was a member of the Althing for thirty years and served at one point as President of that oldest of legislative bodies, founded in A.D. 930 Chairman of the committee which garnered home rule from Denmark in December 1918, his political career was devoted to the struggle for Icelandic political independence. This was instilled in his children and grandchildren. As a result, there was always a lively interest in political matters in the poet's home as he was growing up.

One of the sharpest of youthful memories is of his father bringing home a workman to install a flagpole so that the Icelandic flag could be flown in front of the family home to celebrate full Icelandic independence on 17 June, 1944. The uniqueness of Iceland and the glories of its cultural heritage were an inspiration to the boy throughout his youth. This love of country was reflected in the first poem written by the nine year old poet-to-be:

Ísland þú ert meðal	Iceland, you are among the
fagra landa	beautiful countries
milli stranda.	from shore to shore.
Fjöllin há	The mountains are high
Vötnin blá	the lakes are blue.
Jöklarnir hvítir	The glaciers are white
og mennirnir nýtir.	and the people are able.
Norðurljósin á	The northern lights roam
himni sveima	the heavens
á Íslandi á ég heima	in Iceland, where I live.

As a useful counterbalance, the poet was also made aware of his Norwegian ancestry and encouraged to preserve a romantic linkage with Norway as a mother country. A painting which hangs in his house depicts a flag being flown at half mast, commemorating the death of Nordal Grieg, the Norwegian poet.

One of Johannessen's earliest published poems concerned a five year old child mortally ill with scarlet fever. This was autobiographical. The doctors had told his parents that he was about to die and he was aware of their judgment. Having been under a sentence of death was something he never forgot. But defying expectations, he recovered. One of his poignant memories is of the subsequent destruction of all the personal effects in his room by order of the public health authorities, for fear of spreading contagion. Unfortunately, this included the burning of several small paintings sent to brighten his convalescence by his aunt Louisa Matthíasdóttir, later to become one of Iceland's most famous painters, now living in America.

One of the great sorrows of Johannessen's childhood was the separation of his parents. It was perhaps his adolescent suffering over this separation which transformed him into a poet. It certainly made him very lonely. He had 'long talks with himself' and, at the time — in his words — 'was quite critical of God.' The gossip about the separation was torture for him. Reykjavík was a small town in those days and divorce was uncommon. This episode ended happily with the return of his father to his family. The marriage became stronger as the years wore on. 'My parents lived a very good autumn,' he says.

His father, Haraldur, was a genuine bibliophile. The depression hit Iceland hard and there was not a great deal of money available in the Johannessen family. But whatever there was went to the purchase of books. As a boy, Matthías read most of the volumes in his father's extensive library. He recalls reading Ibsen's collected works in

Norwegian when he was sixteen. But even as a young child his greatest love was the old Icelandic poets. Since Icelandic is a language which has changed remarkably little over the past thousand years, the entire range of Icelandic literature — beginning with the eddas and the poems of the great tenth-century bard Egill Skallagrímsson — was open to him.

Each night, as children will, before going to sleep he said his prayers with his mother. When finished, she would make the sign of the cross over him and then would teach him psalms of Hallgrímur Pétursson, the seventeenth-century priest who became perhaps the most beloved of all Icelandic poets. When he was eight years old Matthías learned that there was a bust of Hallgrímur Pétursson outside Iceland's national cathedral. He recalls walking to the church to look at Hallgrímur's face. One of his fine poems describes Hallgrímur Pétursson chiselling the name of his young daughter, who had just died, on her tombstone.

At sixteen, Johannessen submitted his first poem for publication to the committee that was in charge of producing a volume to commemorate the hundredth anniversary of the founding of the Reykjavík Junior College, which he was attending at the time. The poem was rejected. After that sobering experience he wrote much, but printed only very few poems, which he now regards as a great blessing in disguise. The experimental and tentative manuscripts of his youth were burned.

Although raised in a middle-class home where both his parents were staunch supporters of Independence Party leader Ólafur Thors (Johannessen later wrote a best-selling biography of Thors), the poet as an adolescent was attracted to the egalitarian idealism preached by the Marxists, as expressed by two of the greatest Icelandic writers of the 1930s and 1940s, Thórbergur Thórdarson and Halldór Laxness. (The latter has long since recanted his communist beliefs.) But this youthful flirtation ended when, aged sixteen, he served as a crew member on an Icelandic ship transporting frozen fish from Reykjavík to Leningrad. His visit to the Soviet Union took place in 1946, at the height of the post-war Stalinist crackdown. He immediately felt a great kinship for the Russian people — for their suffering and for the richness of their spirit; Russian literature remains one of his passions. But the political system and the terror that he sensed all about him filled him with loathing. Based on this experience he has written many articles and a historical novel, *Spunnið um Stalín* (Weaving About Stalin).

Individualism under the safety net of a welfare state is

what he now believes in. 'Revolutions always make things worse than they were before the revolution occurred. The best government is a government where friendship counts and where good people help each other. For me, friendship is sacred,' he says.

Johannessen qualified for an advanced degree at the University of Iceland in 1955 in Icelandic philology and literature. He then went to Copenhagen to pursue further studies in world literature and drama. While still at the university, he began working for *Morgunblaðið* — by far Iceland's most important national newspaper, the equivalent of *The Times* and the *Manchester Guardian* combined — and then became its correspondent in Copenhagen. He did this only to earn a living. His aim in life was always to be a poet and a man of letters. He never thought of journalism as a lifetime profession. But in 1959, when not yet thirty years old, Johannessen was offered the prestigious position of editor-in-chief of *Morgunblaðið*. It was an offer he could not refuse. He has been there ever since.

Johannessen is married, and he and his wife Hanna have two sons. Johannessen's first book, published in 1958, was in his academic field, a book about Njáll's saga. The same year he published his first volume of poetry, *Borgin hló* (The City Laughed). Then he wrote a book of interviews with Thórbergur Thórdarson, published in 1959. 'Many people were amazed that I wrote about a Marxist. I don't mind Marxists if they are more interesting than people who agree with me. Thórbergur was the pioneer of Icelandic prose in this century. He taught me a lot about writing. We became great friends.'

One of the things that Johannessen admired most about Hallgrímur Pétursson was the use of daily language, dialogue, and speech rhythms in his poems. This was unique in seventeenth-century Icelandic poetry. In fact, it was not until two centuries later that another great Icelandic poet, Jónas Hallgrímsson, utilized similar techniques. An ardent admirer of these two poets, Johannessen always wanted to write poetry in language which reflected the way people really talk.

> 'But it is very difficult to write like that in Icelandic because we are so influenced by the literary dialogue of the sagas, which is very different from daily speech. It is hard to find a happy ground in between. Icelandic is a very difficult and stiff language, but it has a very cultivated tradition. The language and culture have endured intact despite very strong foreign influences and I think this is very precious. To the Icelander the entire range of his literature is contemporary

literature. It is good for us, who are so few, to have so many alive in our literature. For me poetry is a journey from one idea and thought and place to another. Icelanders have always been able to conquer their misery by conjuring up new worlds which they can shape themselves in their imagination.'

The first modern poet to have profound influence on Matthías Johannessen was Steinn Steinarr — a small, slight, sardonic man with a withered arm, the first twentieth-century poet to break away from the traditional, highly involuted forms of Icelandic poetry.

'I got acquainted with Steinn Steinarr when I was twenty years old and one of the editors of the cultural magazine *Stefnir*. Steinn had not published for some years. He gave me a poem, 'Landsín', and I was very proud to be able to publish it. The poem was big news in cultural circles. I did an interview with him for *Morgunblaðið*. After that, the bourgeois in Reykjavík were more at ease with him. Although a communist in the 1930s, he had grown to hate communism. Steinn had been to Russia. This changed his mind completely. He read the entire manuscript of my first book, *Borgin hló* and became my first literary mentor.'

When Steinarr died at forty-nine in 1958, Tómas Guð-mundsson took over as Johannessen's mentor. Guðmundsson, perhaps the greatest Icelandic poet of this century, was a highly cultivated man with an impeccable ear for the cadences of his language. Although a much more traditional poet himself, he nevertheless recognized Johannessen's gift. In fact, it was he, as editor of *Helgafell*, Iceland's most important literary magazine, who in 1952 printed Johannessen's first published poem. Matthías has written a book on Tómas Guðmundsson, in the form of an interview, and several articles about Steinn Steinarr. Johannessen to this day maintains the practice of having a mentor to curb the quickness of his pen. That role has recently been assumed by Kristján Karlsson, 'whom I consider my literary advisor and a very fresh and strong poet.'

As are all Icelandic poets, Matthías Johannessen is steeped in the cultural traditions of his country. But what makes him fairly unusual is his wide acquaintance with foreign poetry, foreign literature, and foreign authors. And where he is different from many other Icelandic poets is that he draws inspiration from subjects outside of Iceland itself, such as the Verdun battlefield. When quite young he became acquainted with the poetry of Dylan Thomas and wrote the first article on Thomas in Icelandic. He also read Eliot and Pound in his youth and was strongly influenced by Walt Whitman.

'Although much of this poetry was difficult to absorb, we were never the same after having read these poems because they were so different from Icelandic literature. Whitman, Eliot, Dylan Thomas — we paid a visit to their poems and they gave us something which we could use in the long trip onward.

Later I got acquainted with Borges and was fascinated by the man and by his works. He has definitely taught me many things. I met Auden and wrote an article about him. I am familiar with his work and especially gained from meeting and talking to him about literature and culture. Also at that time I was very impressed to meet Faulkner, whom I wrote about. As a young newspaperman I met Arthur Miller and wrote about him as well. I met him again, along with Edward Albee, when I was in New York at a PEN Club meeting. I loved to hear them talk and disagree about everything, except the hallucinations of the critics.

When I think about it, all of a sudden I realize that I have met quite a few interesting people. But lately I have been very preoccupied studying old Icelandic literature and trying to figure out who wrote it and how they did it. It is hard to imagine a newspaperman who has his mind somewhere a thousand years ago, but I am used to being two or three persons at once. And sometimes these persons have to talk to each other and they each gain something from the experience. We could make a poem which would begin "I am not schizophrenic, not yet." Gradually, I am digging more and more into this soil in which my roots are nourished.

You know, I also wrote a book on Halldór Laxness and we have worked together and this has given me great pleasure. I admire his work enormously and I think that he is the man who works most like those who wrote the Icelandic sagas — more than anybody else — and I am of the opinion that Halldór Laxness writes edited history which becomes great poetry. This is the same method that the old unknown author of the sagas used and I have used this method of Laxness to analyze for myself how these old masterpieces were worked out.'

There is no country in the world where poetic traditions and knowledge of poetry is more widespread than they are in Iceland, where poetry is still read not just by a handful, but by the average person. Over the past century more books of poetry have been published in Iceland than books of fiction. The heroes of the Icelandic nation are its poets. It is therefore possible for Matthías Johannessen to hope that his poetry will change the way ordinary Icelanders look at the world, and thus change their lives. Since his audience is broad, he is writing not to reach other poets or titillate those few critics who devote themselves to poetry, which is more and more the case in English and American poetry, but rather to express the most fundamental hopes, fears and thoughts which are universal to all mankind. It is this search for universals which puts him in the mainstream of world literature.

Matthías Johannessen has published twelve volumes of poetry. With each volume he becomes a stronger poet. Widely recognized in Iceland and more and more recognized in Scandinavia, Johannessen is almost unknown elsewhere. He has read and approved each of the translations in this volume, the aim of which is to give the reader of Icelandic a broad selection of his output over the past twenty-five years and to introduce this wide-ranging poet and remarkable man to the English-speaking world.

Marshall Brement
Reykjavík
January 1988

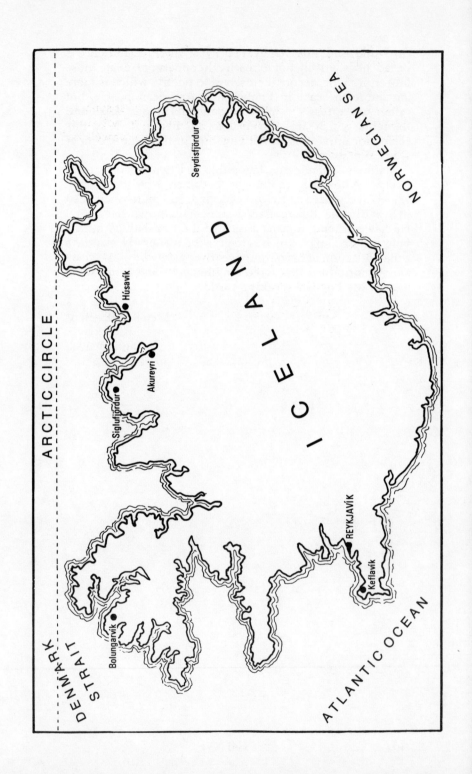

Pronunciation of Icelandic

Icelandic words invariably are stressed on the first syllable. Accents over vowels in Icelandic are therefore not stress marks, as no stress marks are needed. Accented vowels are pronounced as follows:

á	Corresponds to the *ow* in 'fowl'
é	Corresponds to the *ye* in 'yes'
í	Corresponds to the *ee* in 'see'
ó	Corresponds to the *o* in 'hope'
ú	Corresponds to the *oo* in 'food'

There are four extra letters in the Icelandic alphabet.

þ	Corresponds to *th* in the word 'think'
ð	Corresponds to *th* in 'the'
æ	Corresponds to the *i* in 'bite'
ö	Corresponds to the vowel sound in 'word' or 'bird'.

The Poems

Dans

Í hvítum höndum
speglast andlit þitt
eins og ástfanginn máni
í augum þeirra
sem leituðu hamingjunnar,
tvö ein

í hvítum höndum
sem geyma leyndardóm okkar:

hungruð augu
sem gleyptu andlit þitt,
þegar þú teygðir fram barminn
í leit að þyrstum vörum,
tryllt augu,
þegar þú steigst fyrstu sporin
og söngst
mjúk og stinn eins og mjaðarjurt
flöt og hál eins og lúða,

dansandi sígaunaaugu,
þegar ég kom til þín,
maður annarrar konu
þegar ég kom til þín
með svarta sorg í hjarta
og heita þrá í hendi.

Og við dönsuðum.

Og ég dansaði inn í þig,
inn í brjóst þín
og sótti æskuna inn í augu þín,
tíndi mjaðarjurtir
tíndi allt sem þú áttir
gaf þér allt sem ég átti
allt:
    Svarta sorg.

Svo hlógum við,
tvö ein.

2

Dance

Your face is reflected
in white hands
like a love-struck moon
in the eyes of those
who searched for happiness,
two alone.

In white hands
which kept our secret:

hungry eyes
which swallowed your face,
when you leaned forward
in search of thirsty lips,
raving eyes,
when you took your first steps
and sang
soft and resilient as the meadowsweet
flat and slippery as a halibut,

dancing gypsy eyes,
when I came to you,
another woman's man
when I came to you
with black sorrow in my heart
and hot longing in my hand.

And we danced.

And I danced into you,
into your breasts
and fetched youth from your eyes,
picked meadowsweet
picked all that you had
gave you everything
everything:
    Black sorrow.

Then we laughed,
two together.

3

Black Cat

She looked at me like a black cat
with yellow eyes
standing at my feet
wanting to be stroked.

She looked at me
with white transparent eyes
and there was silence between us.

Then I stroked her.

The City Laughed

Do you remember, standing by the lake
looking into your face
the sky reflected in your eyes
deep and thirsty like the laughter of the girl
who came to you with white teeth
like a tern diving for stickleback.
Then night came
and the last wave carried
your shadow ashore
and a new day broke.

Do you remember, the city talking with you
understanding the street laughter
the happiness of the people dancing
to the screaming bassoons, the off-key violins
which stretched into your soul
like the thin fingers
of the young girl at the bar:
you laughed, sang,
but did not see, when darkness sneaked into your faces
and the night moved with soft hands
along fire-red lips.

And the city laughed in your hearts.

Do you remember, an unknown woman coming into your house
and retrieving your youth, picking flowers from hot lips,
and giving you in return the laughter of a child
which filled your ears like surf by the blue cliffs
or the breeze in a green hollow.
You found out that none escapes the city
which he has inhaled
like the scent of a young woman
and before you knew it new eyes stared at you,
two hands met
two words —

and night kissed the dying autumn flower.

Do you remember, youth bidding you farewell
and running lightly into the city,
standing there with empty eyes
and a shiny widow's-peak reminiscent of the journey
into age and darkness:
night stroked a pale cheek
and a forehead, which once felt the flame from thirsty lips,
night passed a cold hand
through the leaves of the trees, and they fell
to the deep autumn-red soil,
and before anyone knew it lonely trees stood
along black asphalt streets,
old trees with naked, colourless branches
— cold, stiffened fingers
which pointed questioningly at those who passed by,

while the city laughed.

Duelling Poems
(Fragments)

You
are the evening sun
on the heath.

Lighting up the darkness
in the obsidian-black eyes
of a night traveller
resting under a frost-sky
who gazes at the houses at dusk
looks at the mountains
taking off their clothes
until they lie
calm-blue and naked searching
for a new crew-cut day
breaking out from the prison of time
when dawn comes

and shouts: Oh, Sun!

You
are a world war
on the sea around Iceland
which was none of our business
we only saw it now and then
when the ships came to the pier
like grey clouds
newly arrived from the sea
for a short stay:
wounded, dead
were carried ashore
but we went home
with tin soldiers in our pockets.
In the field around the church
of Christ the King

many battles were waged
with Ferdinand the bellringer
who had, so we thought,
a lethal weapon in his beard
and the grey hulk of the church was outlined against the sky
like a warship on a blue sea
and in its chancel a red light burned
day and night

and looked to us like a lighthouse
when they brought the dead seamen
in the middle of the game.

Earth from the Sea
(Fragments)

IV

We weave, we weave the web of fate
We weave the children of the land into a poem:

We are our children,
blood flows into the grass
blood colours the grass.

Oh Earth, how you have preserved
our footsteps and remained faithful
to curious eyes.

Our eyes are birds
which fly into the night
our eyes are white migrating birds
searching for a new day.

We are our children.

When death removes
our cross
and we have stopped calling
Barrabas
they will follow our footsteps

they will follow our footsteps.

Oh this respectable cold, the evening-red mountains
the snow black as your eyes
which sowed your love into my heart
and gave me a body: a communion wafer which melted
on my tongue,
I remember how your love bore the scent of communion wine
remember how they glanced at me

as I walked each day with my altar-look
to meet you, filled your ears with honey
and sewed a new spring into you.

You
are a red sailor-suit
and a face with two question-marks:

The Sunday dressed in finery
of yellow leaves
which blew among the dead flowers
and caught in our hair
like the soft fingers of a little girl
caught and then blown out into the morning
to return and follow us

down Harbour Street
and vanish when the ships appear
the grey, black and white ships
in the green brackish water.

Some loaded to the gunwales
like a pregnant woman
impatient to give birth
and to dance
on the blue waves of temptation.

Others empty and sterile
dirty and black and rust-streaked
where the white streaming water gushed
ceaselessly:

I was thinking
that in this way life ran purposeless out into eternity
when I was startled by a question from my son:
'Why do ships piss so much, Daddy?'
and old, experienced Sunday plucked the leaves off itself
like an old woman removing the pins from her dishevelled hair
and smiled kindly at us.

Then our life grew out of the tired days
like a winter-yellow moon from the bulk of Mount Esja:

She remains in a long-forgotten poem
bade farewell to my life as the waves leave a stone,
the land and I, we loved her alone
young and green as the mown grassland.

Yet she has gone. The sun kisses the edge
of sleepy mountains when the day ends —
the woods yawn, young dancing fires
create their poems and pull up the moon:

not knowing that the spring dies with the cut grass,
not knowing that the blue mountains will become grey.

We have called heaven as a witness
to our journey to old cities —
we have bought pictures of Mary in Notre Dame
naked pictures in Pigalle, asked the way
to the Brandenburg Gate, been astonished
in the winter palace of Peter the Great,
looked at the flashing advertisements
in Piccadilly, but God does not advertise there
any more than in *Morgunblaðið*
so we returned home
and became crucified
to the typewriter.

Oh my land, how you have forgiven
our blood in the grass
and given rest to rotten bones
under grey moss.

We two under grey moss.

When the mountain rises
out of the fog-bank, the land thirsts
for a misty sun which stretches
into the frosted winter home-field in our soul
leaves a drop of hope
on the icicles of December words
then: the snowstorm pounds
on empty directionless windows
becomes the jewellery of the earth
and the shadows of the houses run into hiding
before the voice of the war
shouts a judgement over the pathless
fugitives who crawl into the darkness
like worms into the soil —

We are fugitives:

On long nights we wait
for the snowstorm to end and the sun
to give shelter once more against the hail
oh my land, we who are here on a journey
by pure coincidence
and have called upon ourselves the judgement
of the hydrogen bomb,
listen, listen a gust is coming
of a new ice-age which sneaks up on us
on the shoes
of a moving glacier: age of winds, age of wolves.

But we do not have to worry.
Night will pass as it always has,
we will find a new shelter
when the sun comes again:
sends the spring against death
coming from the East brandishing destruction
and puts out the lights
in the churches —

Oh my land, this merciless century
how its shouting dies in the field
which bears our footsteps, this soil.
But we await
the coming of an untamed spring
after this long war

a kicking foal runs into our poem.

We Two

We two
and the surf on an open coast:

to love is to die, sang the surf
death is delusion, said the cliffs
love is a mirage, whispered the poet within us
love goes up to Heaven like distant islands,
you must not come near, you must not touch God's painting.
He takes his job seriously, like Monet,
we remember them under the wall of the church,
there was neighing in the distance
and he looked at her thirsty as Ash Hill
drinking the dregs of the evening sun,
she looked at him and we felt
that this bittersweet moment was a lump in her throat
she longed for him, her yearning
as heavy as the river below the bend,
the church-wall shadows are curious
the eyes in the tramps' faces are dangerous,
I address all of you in my poem
who loved each other as we do:

two alone
your hair ripples over my hands
like water in darkness.
It was a cold winter day
when I said goodbye
a grey sky
like the gable of an old house . . .

Poppy

Yesterday you wore a flowered morning dress with a white
                                                    hairband
today a red sweater which fell tightly against your breasts
and a red silk band around your hair.
In this way you colour the mundane grey days
and make them memorable like the autumn-rue
or the buttercup, which gives our crevice-black surroundings
a warm and etched expression, or the white dandelions
like hair of the land turning grey with autumn
and awaiting the mountain-fresh wind, the gnawing
years which deepen the wrinkles in our faces —
and you do not have to fear the squall
who are not a dandelion in the lee of the autumn
but rather a poppy enclosed and sheltered:
my heart.

Advent

Glittering lightbulbs
on old trees
in forgotten gardens —

Chaste, tired faces
of young shopgirls
with worm-eaten boredom in their answers —

Good intentions
in the eyes of a father of six
who intends to go home after drinking at the Naust —

A Norwegian Christmas tree
by the front yard of a white church
with the moon in its highest branches —

Young sex-tired women
with faces full of Autumn
and washed-out personalities —

A Salvation Army soldier
with white palms and unrequited love:
My Dear Sir, make the pot boil —

Women with religion
and cramps under their bulging shoulder-blades
tread water on the pavements —

A bazaar in a ghostly wooden house
in a dark lot,
cans and empty bottles —

Expectant children
with stuffed stockings
and far too white-bearded guests in their dreams —

Peaceful Coexistence

XVI

When we look at the beach,
and listen to it breathing,
and see its breast heighten
with underwater rocks and seaweed-brown skerries,
we think of you
who bob on a deep
green sea,
fleeing time, fleeing moment, place,
fleeing your blood, land
chained to slogans
of outworn books, in prayer
we think of you
who search for new lands
where the wave plays
with the shining wing, the bird
free and independent
like the words of old people
friends of the soil,
the fruitful Earth, the sun —
rising every day
from the dark depths,
new Earth
fertile.

The Wheat and the Sickle

II

1. Old manuscript,
    pages, letters.
    And words.

    Time
    writes the manuscript
    slowly, deliberately
    at an old desk.
    Still it does not
    exist.

    It writes
    writes
    without seeing,
    and yet sees everything,
    knows everything,
    writes the manuscript
    industriously
    incessantly,

    writes . . . writes . . .

    Odinn sits
    and writes our life
    in the sand —

    sees with one eye,
    with the sun
    during the day,
    the moon at night.

    Writes
    on yellowed pages.

2. The years,
    greeting,
    come toward us,
    now they are dead
    into the ocean.

Still they continue
to murmur
in our blood.

3.   Our blood is an ocean,
     in the ocean
     with the knowledge of those
     who had like us: winds
                         fire
                         and water —
     they who were here on a journey
     they who murmur
     in our blood: Odinn
                    Thor
                    and Loki.
     and Zeus gazes
     from the peak
     over the wide sea.

4. Someone is standing by the deep water,
    peering into the transparent
    depths.

    We have seen
    his shadow
    go past,
    seen him
    cast his net.

    Ensnared:
    We.

We

1

We who are living —
We who are borne by pulsing time
through the arteries of the city,
the concrete city
which drowns the secret gables
of lost ruins —
we who came
despite their voice in our blood,
we who forgot
despite their footsteps:
now even
ferns and forget-me-nots
have stopped growing
by the mossy walls,
their life sealed off
by that stamp of time:
black asphalt.

2

We who no longer understand them
when it is pouring buckets in the Westfjords
and they say: 'Not too dry now, by God'
We who no longer say:
'It's a fair wind from the south'
when a ship sails
through the roughest seas
we who have forgotten
their voice
we who no longer listen
when asked what's new:
'Are they squabbling again like hens?'
why don't we listen?
why don't we search for their footsteps
under the asphalt
where the quiet stream
once ran
and daisies grew in the front yard?

3

But we
who no longer hear
their voice within ourselves
look to heaven
for any hope
of unexpected news.
And everything has changed:
space, time, truth
have lost their meaning
and even their meaning
and even the sewage
is not the same
it has changed canals
and now runs freely
through our veins.

We have forgotten the old stories.

4

Oh, we —
naked machines,
machines within machines —
we who have stopped
quaffing the scent of heather,
and the silence of the heath —
we who have stopped
feeling the sound of the glacier
in our blood
and go wide-eyed
if someone points and says:
God, that dappled horse is beautiful —
we who fill our lungs
with carbon dioxide
and watch the sewage
flowing out of concrete pipes
to the sea.

Oh, we naked machines
who carry the sewage
in our blood
to the sea.

5

We who search for each other
do not find each other
do not hear each other
do not see each other's footsteps
in the asphalt
in the gutter.
We are alone,
alone in this dark snow-storm
which out of old habit
is called life
alone —
without understanding
without seeing
without hearing
alone
without finding each other.

Yet we love each other
like cuckoos
who lay their eggs in the nests of other birds
and leave their young
with strangers.

We go alone
into the blue distance
of unborn dreams,
without knowing each other
without understanding each other
without hearing each other
without finding each other
without having time
to make nests for ourselves
like other birds.

24

6

And we still continue
to search for each other,
and to know of each other
like the stars
which only flicker
in the darkness.

In the darkness
we know of each other,
in our uneasiness
in our suffering
in our sorrow.
When we are alone
in the darkness
we know of each other
we hear each other.

And the sun rises within us
a bright day
but we lose each other
moving into the light,
we lose each other
in the daily joy
the daily weariness
we lose each other
like stars that have stopped flickering,
stars which patiently await
the darkness —

Oh we who only exist
in the darkness.

7

Why? we have
asked.
Where? we have
asked.

Streams flow
under the asphalt
footsteps are lost
under the asphalt
voices become silent
under the asphalt.
Why? we have
asked.
We who search for each other —
we who lost each other
along life's road:
black asphalt.

When the smoke stopped coming
from an old woman's house
it was said:
'Now she's passed on.'

The smoke has stopped coming.

Thingvellir by the Öxará

1

Finally
they cannot say
that our sorrow
would be out of place
in this poem,

when our laughter
is now burnt ashes.

2

the earth has
grown over
the spot where they took away
the tombstone
covered with old and grey
moss

grass and green heather
grow into our wound.

3

This inscription is embossed,
it comes toward us
— the memory comes to us
out of the silence.

4

And the Öxará
flows onward,
this same water
still flows
which we waded
one day
a thousand years ago
last week.

Still this same water
not thinking about death,
not knowing about life —
flowing here
to teach us
to die.

5

The tombstone rises,
the black hands
of the cliffs
grow to heaven.
It is quiet here
only birds and flowers
and people
who receive flowers
from these congealed hands,

in spite of everything.

6

We come here
and celebrate this lava
which once was fire,
this memory
which once was question
joy, burning suspicion.

We search here
where the memory congealed
on its road
between fire and lava,
on its road from you
to us.

Encore at the Arts Festival

Renata Tebaldi
is singing in the Sport Palace,
she has red
hair
she is in a green
dress
the only one in the whole
place
with red hair
in a green dress.
We listen
clap
and get many encores
and the concert also costs
5,300 dollars
that's a lot of money
I mean nowadays
at the same time
that a codblock
has dropped from 82
to 60 cents.

Our father
let the codblocks rise
so that we can get
more encores.
Then Renata Tebaldi could
raise her voice
at no cost to us
with red hair,
like the autumn heather at Thingvellir,
this green thrush.

News from Abroad
(In Short)

1

And the earth is still
barren and empty

And darkness hovers
over the deep.

And God said:
Let there be light.

Now nobody says anything.
Oil crises:

Pisces and Cambyses
get aureoles in their buttonholes.

2

Is it a dream or reality
this Watergate:
that is exactly what
           nobody knows.

Now they have moved this militant Nixon
out of the White House:
He debunked the female fortune-teller Dixon.

3

In the war between the pagan turks
and St. George
which was waged in great heat
on the boundaries of Nicosia
and Famagusta

nothing resulted of course
except
that the renowned Pericles
rhymes with
Clerides.

4

Haile Selassie is in prison
in Addis Ababa,
he wanted to kill everybody.
And there is another Abbysinia
which will never win ya:
the lion is caged and the land ruled
by another hyena.

Sally,
who was Haile Selassie,
Sally?

Women of Iceland

Woman
who keeps the fire going in the oven
of your heart
of despised name
the only proletarian class
of society
which will never
be recognized
the legislators say
and other Christmas party jukeboxes
who put red stockings in the window
on election day;

Woman
who carries her child
inside her
moves her home
to the sounds of spring,
questioning hands
fumbling eyes,
the season of birth
yet does not fill others' nests
with the young of the cuckoo
because of no interest
in nest-building;

Woman who lives
with her children
like the trees with the birds,
with these burgeoning poets
and inquiring philosophers
and unanswered question-marks;

Woman who is a slave to her love
and to her doubt,
slave to her joy
and fostering hands
slave to her affection
and to her mother-heart:
call me again your slave;

Woman
who wakes the household
at daybreak,
scrubs the floor
washes the dishes
washes the half-stopped toilet
washes handkerchiefs and piss-yellow underpants
and hangs her love
out on the line, where it may freeze
in the hard winter frost,
just as she washes a child's bottom
she guards the reputation
of him who netted her
during the great herring rush
at the New Year's dance
in the sports hall;

Woman
who does the dirty work
for shit and lemonade
and asks herself
why?
Feeling good, she denies
that she will be a dishrag
a sponge and a doormat all her life
she asks: What is life
a pain in the ass
and seeks comfort in this
good mood
unpaid proletarian,
identityless
— not even worth a deduction;

Woman
who waits for
life's evening
respected and loved
and too late
looks back
sees a young girl
with soft flaxen hair
eyes smiling like suns
reminders of a broken sentence:
Your eyes shining . . .

Woman
given to Njáll when young
and walks with him
from one fire to another,
he of the scraggly beard,
lives half a century
with some lousy old man
who was only allowed to live
by some colossal misunderstanding;

Woman
who is above all
I am sorry
but God be praised
a Woman

Spider Love

She lies on the window pane
notices everything,
waits:
in the web seven dead flies.

Soon you will be
the eighth.

(5 Rue Amat, Geneva)

Poem of a Man with a Stick

The morning stepped
aside for a young girl
and smiled warmly
sun in hand,
greeted an ailing parliamentarian
who has all his life
leaned his stick on the letter
(in its literal meaning)
began talking with him
eye to eye,
but at home a bearded poet
viewing the new day
which rhymes with the future,
started so alone
(as poets do in their work)
and leaned on his alliterative stick
plunging into uncertainty.

In the story of Audun of the Westfjords
the pilgrim treads
the old man's path
as long as Icelandic
is spoken,
we will travel
from one idea to another.

The Leaves Fall

How the leaves
beat their wings
hopelessly into the packed snow,
How the trees look
with regret
on songless winter
spreading a white embrace
on the past summer,
how it falls
from autumnal branches
which still keep
their red berries
and hungry birds.

How the cats await their prey
all around us.

And the leaves, these broken-winged
hopes, how they are tossed
into a mountain-wide embrace

The Trackless Sea

I

You are the turning point
in my life
I am the flood and the neap tide
and the rhythm of the sea
in your movement.

You came like the sun
across the southern sky
and brought fire to the lakes
and the coarse lava

And secretly my heart was filled
with your beauty

II

A smile
the rock-eyes fill
with strange light
a smile
the deep rivers
become blue from your light

III

From your nearness
my silence has grown
and the sun solders the sky
to the sea,
my eye followed
your eye

That night when nobody slept

IV

You are a smile
you are spring
you are a spring-cool smile

You are the sun
you are the summer
you are the summer sun

You are a year
you are eternity
you are an eternal year

V

You are
a mysterious French
clippership sailing
with sun-stretched canvas
into my consciousness

Hush and be still
here there is much to fear

And the blue reflects the sea
just as the blue of your eyes reflects your youth

VI

We started
on a long uncertain journey
with few provisions.

When I was young
I fell in love
with your innocence

And the wind picks
leaf after leaf
from the birches
and as you can see

The winds of autumn attacked
my heart

And soon the tide will be
coming in

VII

The swords
clang
under the wings of eagles
suns disappear
falling cinders
behind the clouds
and your eyes
set like the sun

Your eyes are glowing embers
of the fire

Your eyes are flashes
of long-dead stars

VIII

The sea
a curious calm white sea

And then one evening
a tired man
goes out of your life,
an old man
with a golden stick
walks into the earth.

42

A Morning in May

Someone is whispering, high up on the wall is a cross,
                                        outside
the man's hair is bouncing, he is hurrying,
no one knows where his journey
is headed, least of all himself, he
forgets the nails of the man who was fastened
to a cross, but runs toward that which somebody
calls a blue, clear day; one step, one
touch, vague joy, but no one
knows why this trembling, it
courses through the fine strings of his heart;
like the violin bow of spring
stroking old catguts, or
finer strings such as time, alone
he goes toward the sun and
unknown music itches in his every nerve;
spring: that tune always alone
which no one can tell you how to rehearse
the touch of bow and string, one blue
clear day and beneath the sun to see;
flowers slowly coming to visit, a bird
and more flowers and birds, to see
everything under the sun, brightening the earth
the fingers of the light glittering in the water
of the mind; touching the untouchable, still
spring and light intermittent flash throughout that day
when the flowers come to visit, the birds
still landing in his mind, the green home-fields,
meadows: they expand swathed with the scent of spring in the
                                        hard
soil of that heart
of sail-white mountains, farther
and farther into the cliffs
of the mind; spring: those blue shafts
stroke the land itself with the bow of the sun.

43

The land fills the mind of the man who goes
without knowing, somewhere, alone
with flowers and birds which accompany him
to strange dreams, all becoming
one: and he becoming that theme fluttering
from the cross of him who knows that all
is one: who still bows the thorned head, and dies
like the bloody ptarmigan with its summer-colours in its wings,
dies after the heather and the long humming midsummer-night
                                                    dream,
dies far from everything and even himself.

And in that way everything comes together, the masked word,
                                          the touch
of birds and flowers in his mind —
visiting the trackless day of the heather, of the heath
of the water, and flying in open embrace: one
quick spring.

Into the Shell

The two of us walked out of the hospital together,
along the lengthy cellar corridor, I
and my light-fearing inner-self
the scent of spring filled our senses, as though
everything were new: each thought new, each
word, through the fever we had heard
the farmer from Dalir say: the rams tiptoed
among the ewes, but in that way
we were also like incomprehensible
guests in this reputable house, now we walk
upright outside, breathing
a new immutable world which lay down
out of doors like farms beneath a slope
or another shelter, we walk out
shelterless, it was sunny and a black van was waiting
and two handy men pushed another
in front of them along the heavy hospital corridor, we
hurried out into the sun and the spring, six together:
we two, the pallbearers and two toys
of that which finally obliterates everything,
silent witnesses of another experience, unready witnesses
                              unprepared for a journey
without a cross, without thorns. Silent about themselves.
On the floor above was a young black-haired
nurse, with spring-sun in her eyes, they that tiptoe among
the shelterless strangers,
each of them in his lair.

Moonlight Poem in the Life of Theresa and Beethoven

And the pale moon came to visit
silently and slowly, stirred the water
and played with the leaves and the grass
continued alone along the forest path to you
and a Hungarian poem is the violin bow of the evening
stroked these fine strings: a memory
set down like a bird in flight between
still branches and sang within you.
You said it was as though an angel were moving

for one instant along a crumpled yellow leaf

on the rotting earth of the forest,
then you played
improvising on her
violin strings, deep out of the forest silence
this first true melody arrived
and it followed you to the last moment
and evades all the violins of this world
as a promise of another better life.

War and Peace

'But the peasants — how do the *peasants* die?' — Leo Tolstoy

And this long Russian winter, white snow-cover deep
into your thoughts, winter far
as the eye can see, and your footsteps like wounded
animals searching for distant peace, your grooved
life blood-path, it still
fills our eyes, letters, diaries, never
any respite in this introverted landscape, still
far from shelter, the frost-bitten earth
wounded and breathless, a swelling under this
pale white snow, and your path disappears
far away into the open
wilderness; we still peer into the ineradicable
words, thoughts, the snow still is not melting although
spring is in the neighbourhood, the scent of trees follows
you far into the deserts of the only land
which protects its wilderness like a fox
putting its dead chicks under the wings of the
ptarmigan, you two still travelling and the mountain
takes longer to cross, unbroken memory
in our disguised suspicion — and yet, spring
is coming, the snow is melting, the birds sing in the green
leaves, rock in the breeze, candy boats
as big as a man's hands.
The footsteps which disappear
lonely and bloody
melt into the soil
into an endless white wilderness, it opens
in our mind like an inverted flower opening its multi-coloured
petals toward the sun and the spring, you disappear
with the river deep into our consciousness, neither
God nor woman, but only you
together on a journey in our spring-blue heart, disappear
together with the trackless humming of the birds,
the flowers and the water; the rustle of the leaves, the wilderness
dances with the falling waves, all new
no 'psychic experience', shallow longing
for suffering and death — one string,
one note and the wilderness sings, the mountains dress

in green clothing of heather and leaves, walk lightly
and alone along the heath as far
as the eye can see, walk into the earth, getting lost
in the song of the birds and the water; our mind
is filled with scent, the scent of greenery, of words
you two on a journey into undisguised spring, alone
finally, Leo, Sonja — without others looking on, flickering
knife-blades, without guilt or self, God or man.
Only you come home — finally like hunted
birds nesting in our thoughts
with feathered hopes: innocent and pure,
without peace or war in the neutral silence
of this immobile time, finally settled
in our deep consciousness, new experience — and you
the sonata itself on hitherto unknown strings,
the sound in this house, still and always
in disguised, fortified houses; one careless April
day; one feathered, flyable day; he flies
home to Yasnaya Polyana, but then
you are gone; the house stands empty
in the wilderness of the mind, an empty shell
without fish or pearl.

Refrain

I

When the night was bright day
when the trees held hands
when the bird's reflection stirred the water
when the water was reflected in your eyes
when your look was a glint on the waves
when our roots intertwined
when the leaves emerged into the promise of spring,
then there was no darkness
then there was no night
then there was no death.

II

The wind passes over the water
the waves pass over the white mirror
a black shadow strikes the bird from the water
a question passes through doubtful eyes
tearing pain surpasses word and touch
thrushes and wimbrels no longer sing
black skuas peck at your eyes,
life itself visits
inevitable sorrow at the door
and death is in the neighbourhood.

III

We were young together
we listened together
we waited for daybreak together
we felt our eyes in the spring-night fluttering together
we riveted our eyes together
we heard the last melody of spring together
we said farewell to the migrating birds together
we greeted life together
we bore grief together
and death will gather us together.

IV

First many and young
then few and middle-aged
now two and alone:
we hear the buzzing become silent
we see the green leaves become pale
we experience each of life's changes
slowly, inexorably into a transparent dream
and we see those who started with us
changing into moss-grown tombstones.

Was this it then?
were the promises cracked fingerbones
in the cold soil
were we ourselves this spring-bright night
which turned to daylight,
this hope which fossilized?

V

All these days
and dark nights
this jagged incomprehensible pain
this fear in the palm
of unknown destiny.
We too
and yet only
this spring-bright night
the swans flew towards the heath
this spring-bright night.

VI

We have bidden farewell to many coffins
and bowed our heads at many graves
and been silent together.
Yet for a while
we will hold hands and
head together toward an undug grave

51

but until the soil
rests these tired eyes
no defences are possible:
retreat according to plan
from one hope to another.

VII

But darkness seeks shelter
in the trenches
and darkness covers the battlefield
when evening comes.

VIII

And death comes into the face
of another man.

Turning of the Tide

At five in the morning
it gets colder, the birds stop singing
and the bloody war between day and night
hardens, the final battle at this moment
each morning, everything loses
vital force and those awaiting death
die in falcon-grey
houses, a fresh breeze passes through the meadows
and the home-fields, spiritless horses
think their own thoughts in spite of everything
as though expecting
that now the battle will begin,
spiritless horses and birds
of this unbroken silence, of this
morning-cool tide shifting, wait for
light to triumph
and the cool darkness to flee on dusk-black shoes,
night to disappear like a shovel of coal
into the blazing day
with the sun and the fresh breeze
in the eyes of the singing birds of this prepared
land, of the perched morning-blind owl
and it is a long way between the fallen
cairns and time is breathing on the beach
and greeting a mountain-blue day
on your road, my land.

Lennon

I

But you who never became
sixty-four
never anything but a forty-year-old boy
no, a four-year-old
within a grown man,
now before your time
long before your time
you looked into the gunbarrel
and the fang spat poison
into your undefended heart
long before your time: he aimed
at the grown man, preserved
in the fortified heart of a boy
waiting at home for his father, now
never again to take his father's hand
before walking across Central Park West
because you have gone on an unexpected visit
to meet the Gods, you went unexpectedly
to meet the Gods
and in her face,

the sun-smile of the Goddess stopped radiating
in your faces . . .

You who sang about love, about peace
of the boy in your dream, he
who changed the world of searching eyes
into paradise regained
and was not supposed to be afraid
to cry: perhaps he will be
sixty-four one gunless
day he will be sixty-four
in the song of this full-grown child
and the eternal madness of the Beatle and then you will
participate,
Lennon, in the joy of the Gods
engulfed by the advent-smile of the Goddess

who poured rays of hash over your love
when Yoko thought it was as innocent
to sing: 'Hard times are over'
as you and McCartney thought it self-evident that the day
                                        would come
'when I'm sixty-four', and it did not come
no new day comes from a gushing
gun-barrel, still we will hear the powder-smoke
in these intriguing words: 'all we are saying
is give peace a chance,' words, words
powerless memory when the sun-smile of the Goddess
changes into black tumbling darkness.

II

And grieving awakened youth
went with you to meet the Gods
youth old before its time
against the serpent's tongue, death's moment

but we who are sixty-four
in our minds
and we who are sixty-four,
have seen old age fetching our youth, without destiny
in the trash-heap of this cunning time

which catches us in a nylon net,
we have looked at death
fetching our old age from a trash-heap
under soil and grass, we have looked at death
fetching the light in our eyes and disappearing with it
into the brightness of a new, intriguing day —

We expect God to change us into a part
of himself
just as the home-field will become green from
the rotting manure.

III

Oh, Lennon, if our youth
were made of plastic
if our old age and death
were made of plastic
if our happiness and sorrow
were made of plastic
if our poem and song
were made of plastic
if our love and hate
were made of plastic
if our envy and jealousy
were made of plastic
if our hope and expectation
were made of plastic —
we would not have needed
to create God

and would have lived
deathless synthetic lives
made of indestructible synthetic substances
in eternal plastic
in a smooth synthetic world: from plastic
did we come and into plastic we will
return
under an eternal plastic heaven
of this synthetic God that we
would not have needed . . .
If, who says if . . .

synthetic cows
synthetic money
synthetic ideals . . .

And furthermore, Lennon:
synthetic love
synthetic feeling
synthetic peace
synthetic God . . .

And a synthetic smile
in synthetic noise
in a synthetic world
of this synthetic war . . .

If, who says if . . . ?
synthetic crucifixion
on a synthetic Golgotha
under a plastic sun
of these long-dead stars.
And the synthetic cliffs broke apart . . .

No, you shouted
this eternal no too late: and the plastic smile
became a shimmering tear, the worry was dissipated
as was the enticing noise, this calm white silence
after the storm:

And there was love
and there was feeling
and there was peace
and there was God

Crucifixion under the blue
sky of these frightened birds, resurrection: the flesh is
                                        mortal
but resurrection is immortal
the flesh is in weakness
but resurrection is in strength . . .

And a new day peeks
over the mountain's edge
a new day in spite of everything
and his eyes open

half-way, in spite of everything,
and we walked together into the sun-red
west, we walked together
on the water, the dead and the living,
it made no difference,
we walked together on the water

one sweet day which is fading . . .

and the day shuts its half-closed eyes again.

Flýgur örn yfir

(Fragments)

I

Nýrúin fjöll,
það er sumar.

II

Golan hleypur
á tjörnum

og vatnið breytist
í gáruýfða
unga.

III

Hér hefur jökullinn
numið staðar
á leið sinni
til sjávar
skyggnzt um
og hlaðið sandvörður
við veginn

í fótspor hans
fylgir áin,
daggarslóð
í jónsmessuþýfi.

The Eagle Flies Over

I

The mountains are newly shorn,
it is summer.

II

The breeze runs
the surface of the ponds

the water becomes
wave-ruffled
ducklings.

III

Here the glacier
stopped
on its path
to the sea
looked around
and built sand cairns
by the roadside

the river follows
in its footsteps,
midsummer-night hummocks
through the dew-wet grass.

IV

Blátt vatnið
er kvöldrautt
undir sól
þegar jörðin
lokar augum
undir sólstöðukyrran
svefn.

V

Ungir teymdum
við hesta
um sporlausa heiði

fífan
kviknar
við veginn

sól kveikir
fífuhvítastar
júnítýrur
við sporlausan
veginn.

VI

Klófífu-
hvítir
eru draumar okkar,

þessir klógulu
ernir.

IV

The blue water
is evening-red
in the midnight sunlight
when the earth
closes its eyes
in the quiet
of the longest day.

V

When young
we walked the horses
around the trackless heath

the cottongrass
lights
the roadside

the sun brightens
the whitest cottongrass
like fireflies
along the trackless
road.

VI

The white
puff flowers
are our dreams

these yellow-clawed
eagles.

VII

Kvöldlaus
er kyrrðin

flugnasuðs-
laus hnígur
flugumýri
í móa og dröfnótta
spóavængi
krossblóm og fjór-
blaðasmára

en eyjarnar hverfa
með bliki
af báru til hafs

XIX

Hvítir
gagnsæir
skuggar
rísa
úr hafi
til himins

fjöll ganga
óséð
inní marblá
vötn
þinna augna.

XXII

Langur
er þessi koss
sólar og fífils

VII

The quiet
is nightless

the flies
slowly descend
without sound
become the heather and the freckled
wings of the wimbrel
the wildflowers
and the clover

the islands disappear
with the blink
from the wave toward the sea

XIX

White
transparent
shadows
rise
from the sea
toward the sky

mountains walk
unseen
into the sea-blue
waters
of your eyes.

XXII

The sun
gives a lengthy kiss
to the dandelions

gul bros
við veginn.

XXIII

Augu okkar
fljúga
til jökla.

XXIV

Öræfabjört
eru ilmbrún
augu þín

þessi kvöldsvölu
heiðavötn
í fylgd
með svanhvítri
hugsun.

XXV

Klettsvartar
leggjast gárur
yfir freyðandi
strengjaða
hylji
þar sem hugur þinn
leitar sér
athvarfs
fyrir hádegisskugga
holti
og heyrandi nær.

yellow smiles
along the road.

XXIII

Our eyes
fly
towards the glaciers.

XXIV

Your scent-brown
eyes are
wilderness-bright

these evening-cool
mountain lakes
accompany
the swan-white
thought.

XXV

The waves lie down
rock-black
over foaming
cascading
depths
where your thought
seeks
shelter
against the noon shadow
the hill
and the invisible presences.

XXVII

Ósofin
með syngjandi
stelk á fingrum

ilmandi blóðberg
í léttstignu spori

kemur unglingslegur
ljóshærður dagur

með brennisóleyjar-
bros af nývöknuðum

heiðum.

XXXIII

Morgunblöð
á snúru

síðustu fréttir
að sunnan
hengdar til þerris
í þjóðbraut

sólbakaðar fréttir
eins og saltur
fiskur.

XXXIV

Berfætt
á handleggjunum
leika börnin
við garðslöngu
og ánamaðka

XXVII

Sleepless
with a
sandpiper on its fingers

the scented thyme
in the light footstep

the young
blond day comes

with a buttercup
smile from freshly awakened
heaths.

XXXIII

Morning papers
on a clothes-line

the latest news
from the south
hung for drying
at the main road

sun-baked news
like salt
fish.

XXXIV

Barefoot
on their arms
the children play
with a garden hose
and the earthworms

í ánni
vaka lontur og kóð
við kafloðna
bakka.

LII

Andlit þitt
glaðlegt hús
eins og ljóð mitt
glaðlegt hús
með hláturmild blóm
í gluggum.

the fish break the water
by the hairy
banks
of the river.

LII

Your face
a happy house
like my poem
a happy house
with ever-laughing flowers
in the windows.

Other Translations of Matthías Johannessen

Published in Denmark
Klagen i jorden (1968)

Published in Sweden
Karpol är din vinge (1981)

Published in Norway
Ask veit eg standa (1981)
Fra hav til jökel (1975)
Varen kjem ridand (1976)

Published in Finland
Ja tun turin takaa kuulet (1977)

Published in Iceland in English
Kjarval (1974)
Asmundur Sveinsson (1971)
Erro (1978)

Published in Germany
Ultima Thule (1985)

FOREST BOOKS

Special Collection

THE NAKED MACHINE Selected poems of Matthías Johannessen.
Translated from the *Icelandic* by Marshall Brement. (Forest/
Almenna bokáfélagid)
0 948259 44 2 cloth £7.95   0 948259 43 4 paper £5.95   96 pages

ON THE CUTTING EDGE Selected poems of Justo Jorge Padrón.
Translated from the *Spanish* by Louis Bourne.
0 948259 42 6 paper £7.95   176 pages

ROOM WITHOUT WALLS Selected poems of Bo Carpelan.
Translated from the *Swedish* by Ann Borne.
0 948259 08 6 paper £6.95   144 pages. Illustrated

CALL YOURSELF ALIVE? The love poems of Nina Cassian.
Translated from the *Romanian* by Andrea Deletant and
Brenda Walker. Introduction by Fleur Adcock.
0 948259 38 8 paper £5.95   96 pages. Illustrated

RUNNING TO THE SHROUDS Six sea stories of
Konstantin Stanyukovich.
Translated from the *Russian* by Neil Parsons.
0 948259 04 3 paper £5.95   112 pages. Illustrated.

East European Series

FOOTPRINTS OF THE WIND Selected poems of Mateya Matevski.
Translated from the *Macedonian* by Ewald Osers.
Introduction by Robin Skelton.
0 948259 41 8 paper £6.95   96 pages. Illustrated

ARIADNE'S THREAD An anthology of contemporary Polish
Women poets. Translated from the *Polish* by Susan Bassnett and
Piotr Kuhiwczak.
0 948259 45 0 paper £6.95   96 pages.

POETS OF BULGARIA An anthology of contemporary
Bulgarian poets.
Edited by William Meredith. Introduction by Alan Brownjohn.
0 948259 39 6 paper £6.95   112 pages.

THE ROAD TO FREEDOM Poems by Geo Milev.
Translated from the *Bulgarian* by Ewald Osers.
UNESCO collection of representative works.
0 948259 40 X paper £6.95   96 pages. Illustrated.

STOLEN FIRE Selected poems by Lyubomir Levchev.
Translated from the *Bulgarian* by Ewald Osers.
Introduction by John Balaban.
UNESCO collection of representative works.
0 948259 04 3 paper £5.95   112 pages. Illustrated.

AN ANTHOLOGY OF CONTEMPORARY ROMANIAN POETRY
Translated by Andrea Deletant and Brenda Walker.
0 9509487 4 8 paper £5.00   112 pages.

GATES OF THE MOMENT Selected poems of Ion Stoica.
Translated from the *Romanian* by Brenda Walker and
Andrea Deletant. Dual text with cassette.
0 9509487 0 5 paper £5.00   126 pages   Cassette £3.50 plus VAT

SILENT VOICES An anthology of contemporary Romanian women
poets. Translated by Andrea Deletant and Brenda Walker.
0 948259 03 5 paper £6.95   172 pages.

EXILE ON A PEPPERCORN Selected poems of Mircea Dinescu.
Translated from the *Romanian* by Andrea Deletant and
Brenda Walker.
0 948259 00 0 paper £5.95.   96 pages. Illustrated.

LET'S TALK ABOUT THE WEATHER Selected poems of Marin Sorescu.
Translated from the *Romanian* by Andrea Deletant and
Brenda Walker.
0 9509487 8 0 paper £5.95   96 pages.

THE THIRST OF THE SALT MOUNTAIN Three plays by Marin Sorescu
(Jonah, The Verger, and the Matrix).
Translated from the *Romanian* by Andrea Deletant and
Brenda Walker.
0 9509487 5 6 paper £6.95   124 pages. Illustrated

VLAD DRACULA THE IMPALER A play by Marin Sorescu.
Translated from the *Romanian* by Dennis Deletant.
0 948259 07 8 paper £6.95   112 pages. Illustrated.

Fun Series

JOUSTS OF APHRODITE Erotic poems collected from the Greek
Anthology Book V.
Translated from the *Greek* into modern English by Michael Kelly.
0 948259 05 1 cloth £6.95   0 94825 34 5 paper £4.95   96 pages.